the last decade of
SCOTTISH STEAM

the last decade of
SCOTTISH STEAM

DEREK CROSS

BRADFORD BARTON

Frontispiece: The 'Princess Royal' Pacifics were never as common in Scotland as south of Carlisle, but a train that regularly produced one was the down 'Birmingham Scotsman' even as late as 1960, a year before diesels took over these trains. No.46200 *The Princess Royal* attacks the last mile of Beattock in September 1960 with the morning Birmingham – Glasgow train.

OTHER TITLES BY Derek Cross in this uniform series include:

LONDON MIDLAND STEAM OVER SHAP
LONDON MIDLAND STEAM IN THE NORTHERN FELLS
LONDON MIDLAND STEAM NORTH OF THE BORDER

© Copyright D. Bradford Barton Ltd ISBN 085153 3515

Published by Lomond Books
36 West Shore Road, Granton, Edinburgh EH5 1QD

Printed and bound in Great Britain by BPC Hazell Books Ltd

introduction

*'Like some far spent taper, for an instant I recover,
And then instantly go out . . .'*

WEBSTER . . . 'The White Devil.'

That quotation from one of the more gory Jacobean dramas sums up exactly the final decade of the steam locomotive in Scotland. For ten years between 1958 and 1967 the railways of Scotland saw a variety of steam locomotives un-rivalled since the pre-Grouping days. While south of the Border it came more and more a case of Black 5s with everything, in Scotland not only were there a good scattering of pre-Grouping classes but most of the Standard classes as well. Not only that, but far more than anywhere else in the country, Nationalisation meant rationalisation with ex-LNER locomotives appearing on ex-LMSR lines and vice versa. All the larger Standard classes – except, rather surprisingly, the Class 4 4-6-0 – appeared in most parts of the country with varying degrees of success. The Standard 4 Moguls were held in high regard, as were the Standard 5s and the 2-6-4 tanks. The lines of the old G & SW got good work out of the 'Clans' though the work of the 'Britannias' in Scotland was never more than mediocre. In this volume I have illustrated forty-eight classes (and sub-classes) of different steam locomotive: and I don't for a moment claim that this was the whole lot, as any one person can only be in one place at a time. Strange to say, most of these classes could have been seen at one time or another by an observer between Kilmarnock and New Cumnock on the Nith Valley line of the old G & SW. Not withstanding that this was my 'home ground', I have tried to vary the photographic locations as well as the locomotive classes, though inevitably some places crop up frequently as they were the focal points for the greatest variety.

This abundance of differing types was a Scottish phenomenon: for at the Grouping in 1923 there were probably more varieties for the total number of engines within the old Scottish companies than anywhere else in Britain. This also tended to be true at Nationalisation in 1948 as even then odd remnants from the five former Scottish companies were taken into BR stock. Apart from the coming of the Standard designs what made this all the more notable was that the variety of classes was concentrated into the Central Lowlands and South Scotland. 1958 in many ways was the critical year as by then steam had been, or was very rapidly being, phased out over the whole of the Highland and Great North of Scotland system, mainly on account of the shortage of suitable coal locally. The West Highland held on to steam for a year or two longer, but with B1s and the inevitable Black 5s displacing the LNER Moguls and ex-NB 4-4-0s that had been a feature of that line for so long. Also in 1958 dmus took over many of the suburban services and the Edinburgh–Glasgow lines. A year later Class 40 diesels began to appear on some of the Anglo-Scottish expresses, though long before this the LMS twins Nos.10000/1 and the Southern-built diesel-electrics had intermittently worked some of the West Coast services to and from Glasgow.

In a way it was the influx of diesels that gave the stimulus to the final burst of steam workings in Scotland. Main line locomotives displaced by diesels from both the West and East Coast routes began to appear on the most unexpected turns. Probably the best-known example of this was the use of A3s, displaced from the East Coast main line, over the Midland and G & SW route between Leeds and Glasgow. This was not all by any means, LNER Pacifics made frequent appearances on freight traffic over the Waverley Route and also on the G & SW line between Glasgow and Carlisle. Black 5s appeared almost everywhere, though Fife remained staunchly LNER, and in cases North British, until the end. LMS Pacifics were demoted to parcels and fitted freight workings, with more than their share of local passenger traffic on the Nith Valley line. The zenith of this cornucopia of locomotive variety undoubtedly came in the years 1962-64 after which the numbers of steam locomotives in use began to dwindle, though here again the G & SW lines and Fife fought a strong rearguard action. From mid-1965 onwards the numbers of steam locomotives at work in Scotland declined rapidly, though surprisingly enough not their variety. There was the glorious 'Swan song' of the LNER Pacifics on the Glasgow–Aberdeen lines. The 'Crabs' dominated Ayrshire's mineral traffic to the end of 1966 when all steam based in Scotland was officially withdrawn. Various ex-North British 0-6-0s did the same in Fife and it is of interest that the last Scottish-based steam locomotive to work for BR in Scotland was an ex-North British J36 0-6-0 of 1880 vintage that continued working the Seafield Colliery shunts from Thornton in Fife until the end of March 1967. This was three months after all steam had officially been withdrawn, as the Clayton Class 17 diesels provided for such duties had proved pitifully inadequate. The J36s' disappearance was not through any fault of the engines but because 'authority' got to know, and a Class 37 had to be provided instead!

1967 was an anti-climax, as the only steam workings into Scotland were by locomotives based at Kingmoor shed

(Carlisle). To cater for these some servicing facilities were left at certain sheds, notably Polmadie and Perth, Ayr and St. Margarets (Edinburgh). Operational water columns were also maintained at various key stations, though the water troughs on the Caledonian and G & SW lines were lifted. No fresh stocks of coal were carried at the sheds, so by the middle of 1967 engines working north from Carlisle had to have enough coal to get them home again. By the autumn of 1967 the reign of steam in Scotland was over, apart from privately run specials and dire emergencies. It was a spectacular finale especially in the years 1962-64 when traffic was heavy and mainline express engines kept cropping up on the unexpected, in unexpected places. In looking through photographs of this decade one becomes aware of many other changes quite apart from the motive power. The whole railway scene was altering. Signalling was changing; types of stock, both passenger and freight, was changing: the local stations, very often of considerable architectural merit, were being closed and in many cases demolished. Not only this but the whole landscape was changing, combine harvesters did away with orderly rows of stooks in the cornfields, hay ricks vanished before the hungry maw of balers, tower silos sprang up. Urban renewal shot high rise flats like bandaged fingers to the skies. Road widening and renewal scattered brash concrete bridges in place of the old weathered stone ones so much a part of the landscape. The end of the steam locomotive was part of an overall pattern of change, often for the worse, that occurred in this decade. At least in Scotland the steam locomotive went out in style, even if in the inevitable aura of dirt and neglect. It is arguable that the last decade was possibly the most interesting of all the 130-odd years of Scottish steam.

In attempting to show these variations, I admit that I may not have covered them all, and that my geographical coverage is limited to more or less south of Perth. However there is enough here to show the extraordinary variety of locomotive classes that worked in Scotland over the last decade of steam. There were other classes that came 'on passage', as the ornithologists would say—Ivatt Moguls for example appearing occasionally when I never had a camera. 8Fs surprisingly were rare visitors; some classes were withdrawn early in the decade such as the 'Princess Royals' and the big Austerity 2-10-0s. Most 4-4-0s had gone by the end of 1961 and are poorly represented, but against this there were such Scottish peculiarities as domeless Class 5s well into the mid 1960s. Some of these photographs suffer from being taken in poor weather conditions, but there seems to be an un-written law in railway photography that the more interesting the engine, the worse the weather. Finally Scotland was lucky in the imaginative stroke of genius by the then General Manager, James Ness, who anticipated the preservation boom by a decade and restored the famous four examples of pre-Grouping classes to working order in the late 1950s. I have shown these in passing and briefly, as they have been well illustrated many times before. Forty-eight classes of locomotive in the final decade is remarkable by any standards, and very different from the 'Chips (or Class 5s) with everything' that many of us have come to associate with the end of steam.   Derek Cross

'The Lizzies', as the earlier LMS Pacifics were affectionately known to the men, staged their swan song on the morning Euston–Perth express northwards from Carlisle in the summer of 1962, with Kingmoor's trio Nos.46200–3 taking the duty in rotation. No.46203 *Princess Margaret Rose* waits in Carstairs station with this train on 27 August 1962 on her penultimate day of service.

The final form of A3 to work in Scotland had the double chimney, but their appearance was somewhat improved by the addition of 'Austrian' smoke deflectors. In this final form No.60070 *Gladiateur* nears Sanquhar at dawn on 26 July 1963 with an overnight relief from St. Pancras to Glasgow (St. Enoch).

7

By the end of 1962 most of the long-distance Anglo-Scottish expresses were in the hands of Class 40 diesels. The most notable exception was the afternoon Perth – Euston express, seen here at Craigenhill Summit, north of Carstairs, with No.46236 *City of Bradford* in charge, on 4 April 1963.

One of the last, if not the last, regular workings for an LMS Pacific in Scotland was the 5.30 p.m. Glasgow (St. Enoch) - Carlisle semi-fast. On Friday 4 October 1963, No.46242 *City of Glasgow* heads this train round the long curve at Bowhouse, south of Kilmarnock.

The up Royal Scot approaching Gretna Junction off the Caledonian main-line in August 1958 hauled by No.46234 *Duchess of Abercorn.* This photograph, taken about 200 yards north of the Border, shows the full length Royal Scot before the load was reduced to compensate for electrification work south of Crewe. Below: for a short while before going over to diesel haulage, the truncated Royal Scot was still in the hands of the LMS Pacifics. No.46247 *City of Liverpool* plays with its eight-coach load on a dark November day in 1960 in the Clyde Valley between Lamington and Wandel Mill.

Rebuilt 'Scot' No.46108 *Seaforth Highlander*, of Holbeck shed at Leeds, coasts round one of the many curves on the Nith Valley line near Sanquhar with the morning Leeds-Glasgow express. The windblown hayricks in the field are now as much a part of history as regular steam-hauled express trains.

The rebuilt 'Royal Scots' had a long innings on the Midland/G & SW line between Leeds and Glasgow but when this photograph was taken in September 1960 they were about to be superseded by A3s for a short while before the diesels took over; No.46130 *The West Yorkshire Regiment* pulls out of Dumfries with a Saturday extra from Leeds to Glasgow (St. Enoch).

The whole of this scene on 6 April 1961 has gone beyond recall, for electric wires and colour light signals now rule at Beattock Summit. Gone also have the Carlisle-Glasgow stopping trains, the afternoon one seen here ambling over the top of the long bank behind rebuilt 'Scot' No.46102 *Black Watch*.

13

So far as is known, none of the rebuilt 'Patriots' were actually shedded in Scotland and as a result they were never as common as the 'Royal Scots', though were frequent visitors on summer workings to and from the south. No.45545 *Planet* climbs the tortuous length of the Clyde Valley near Abington on 19 May 1961 with an afternoon Glasgow—Manchester express.

The early summer of 1963 in south Scotland was abnormally dry and the last week-end of May was very hot—weather conditions which account for the lack of exhaust from No.45531 *Sir Frederick Harrison* on the final mile of Beattock Bank. Despite the absence of visible exhaust, the engine was working very hard with an unassisted eleven coach train from Manchester to Glasgow on 31 May 1963 and the sparks resulted in some comprehensive bank burning all the way from Greskine to Summit!

In the last five years of Scottish steam, it was the Nith Valley line of the old G & SW that produced the greatest variety of unexpected motive power. On 23 May 1964 the morning stopping train from Carlisle to St. Enoch, seen here near Auchinleck, was unexpectedly hauled by rebuilt 'Patriot' No.45527 *Southport*.

Less than a year later, No.45527 passes the same place in company with 'Royal Scot' No.46155 *The Lancer* towed by Class 5 No.44955 en route from Upperby (Carlisle) shed to the West of Scotland Shipbreaking yard at Troon for scrapping.

The unrebuilt 'Patriots' were never common in Scotland and from 1958 onwards were very rare indeed. The photograph above of No.45544 near Wandel Mill in the Clyde Valley on a miserable September day in 1958, with a Preston—Edinburgh excursion, is the only time that I saw one north of the Border during the last ten years of steam. Below: the Stranraer portion of the famous 5.10 p.m. from Glasgow (St. Enoch) climbing past Alloway Junction, south of Ayr, in September 1958, with a background of corn stooks so typical of pre-combine autumns. The locomotive is No.45718 *Dreadnought* with a small tender. These were paired with some of Corkerhill shed's 'Jubilees' at this date.

An unexpected survival as late as 25 March 1961 was 'Jubilee' No.45662, still with a boiler carrying a combined top-feed, seen here on the Neilston Bank with a Glasgow–Kilmarnock football special. Even more surprising is the fact that No.45662 *Kempenfelt* was shedded at Bristol (Barrow Road) at the time.

The 9.0 a.m. Carlisle–Glasgow stopping train climbing Beattock Bank above Greskine signal box with 'Jubilee' No.45742 *Connaught* in charge, 27 May 1964. This engine at one time carried a double chimney and, along with No.45588, was destined to be one of the last two 'Jubilees' to work regularly in Scotland, the pair surviving at Kingmoor (Carlisle) into early 1965.

No.45589 *Gwalior* nears Polquhap Summit with a Glasgow–Leeds relief to the up 'Thames–Clyde Express' on 3 June 1963. The lack of exhaust is due to the abnormally hot early summer of that year.

One of the specialities of St. Rollox works was to outshop Class 5s with domeless boilers long after the practice had ceased elsewhere. As recently as 29 March 1964 No.45124, obviously not long out of shops, approaches Dalry Junction with a Kilmarnock - Ibrox football excursion. The train is coming off the old G & SW mainline between Dalry and Kilmarnock, now closed and lifted.

Many of the Scottish Class 5s ran with the combined dome/top-feed arrangement, as on No.45010 seen here leaving Dumfries with a stopping train to Glasgow on 22 April 1961.

Domeless Class 5 No.45029, lacking even a top-feed cover, pilots No.45363 of the most common variety (with the top-feed immediately ahead of the dome) on a St. Pancras–Glasgow football special into New Cumnock on 11 April 1965.

A closer look at No.45363 with the most common dome/top-feed arrangement, restarting the St. Pancras – Glasgow football special out of New Cumnock after dropping the pilot on Sunday 11 April 1965.

While to my knowledge there were never any of the Caprotti valve-geared Black 5s in Scotland, Stranra[e]
'borrowed' the Stephenson valve-geared No.44767 for a few months in 1966. This engine, now preserve[d]
and named *Stephenson*, and reckoned by the Stranraer men to be the best of any Class 5, is seen here nea[r]
Kilkerran piloting conventional No.45162 with the morning Stranraer–Ayr express goods in April 196[6]

The ultimate form of boiler on the LMS Class 5s had the top feed immediately behind the smoke-box as on No.44672, seen here about to take water at Dumfries on 19 August 1967. The need for water was due to the removal of the troughs at Mossband and Upper Cairn a year earlier. As far as is known, this was the last steam working of a booked passenger train into Scotland, the train being the Saturday relief to the down 'Thames-Clyde Express', steam-worked on account of a diesel failure at Carlisle.

It has been said that the Hughes/Fowler Moguls (or 'Crabs') were the best engines the LMS ever brought to Scotland and certainly they were used extensively on quite important passenger workings into the 1960s. On 2 June 1962 No.42916, of Ayr shed, restarts the through Heads of Ayr–Leeds (S.O.) train from a signal check at Barassie, the locomotive in this instance working through to Carlisle.

The 'Crabs' latterly were very much Ayrshire engines and worked many of the hardest mineral turns till the end steam there in October 1966. On a frosty 31 January 1966, No.42789 tackles the Crosshill bank near Carsloe Bridge the Girvan Valley with the morning Bargany–Ayr Harbour coal train.

Apart from a short period during the war when some were shedded at Motherwell the Stanier 8F 2-8-0s were never based in Scotland. Indeed in the last decade of steam they were very rare visitors indeed and I personally know of only two instances. One of these was on a drizzly March day in 1964 when No.48612 worked the Shap Quarry–Ravenscraig limestone train, seen here leaving the north end of Beattock Yard.

In 1958, before the coming of dmu's the 2P 4-4-0s were the mainstay of the local services in South-West Scotland such as the Ayr–Dalmellington trains. An evening train from Ayr–Dalmellington is signalled for the branch as it passes Dalrymple Junction, three miles south of Ayr, behind No.40610 in September 1958.

The Ayr–Dunure and Turnberry light railway must have been one of the most scenic in Scotland: though by the time this photograph was taken in the summer of 1958 passenger trains only ran as far as Heads of Ayr to serve Butlin's Camp there. 2P No.40647 passes Greenan siding with one of these trains on an August evening. The track into the siding is still in situ and used for the early potato traffic and the local coal merchant ... who would appear to be in dire need of a new lorry! The telephone pole visible was reputed to be the highest in Scotland.

4Fs were never common in Scotland, though it might be thought that they would have been very suitable for some of the shorter heavy mineral turns. However Hurlford shed (Kilmarnock) had a few from the end of 1958 until late 1961. From time to time Ayr got hold of one of these and frequently used it on the early morning Ayr–Girvan local passenger train, seen here at Alloway Junction in the Autumn of 1958 with No.44331 in charge.

One of Hurlford's 4Fs (No.44281) near Cronberry in April 1961 with a coal train from Muirkirk to Hurlford mineral sidings (Kilmarnock). This engine finished its career shortly afterwards in a stream at the end of a particularly nasty spur in one of the local collieries.

While the large Ivatt Class 4 Moguls were only rarely seen in Scotland, the smaller variety were sprinkled over a wide area ranging from Dundee to Stranraer. On 1 March 1965 No.46413 was photographed passing through Ayr station with the local shunting service—known as 'The Squib' on account of its darting in and out of every siding in the district. No.46413 was an interesting engine as this was the one sent to Swindon for draughting experiments soon after introduction of the class, when there were complaints of poor steaming.

The prize for the most rural line in Scotland must undoubtedly go to the Whithorn branch in Galloway (closed in 1964) and especially the mile-long spur from Millisle to Garlieston. When this photograph was taken in April 1963 there was a thrice-weekly goods service to Whithorn, but once a week was enough for everyone's nerves getting down to Garlieston. Ivatt 2 MT No.46467, with the ugly narrow chimney, returns towards Millisle at the time when these Ivatt 2-6-0s had a monopoly of the line.

Possibly the best-known workings of the Fairburn 2-6-4 tanks during the last decade of Scottish steam was as bankers on Beattock; On 25 July 1964 No.42125 assists a Liverpool–Glasgow train past Greskine box. A very rare visitor to Scotland, ex-Crosti boilered 9F No.92024 waits in the refuge siding with a northbound goods.

The coming of the dmu's to most of the Scottish outer suburban services between 1958 and 1961 spelt the end of the once-numerous workings of the Fairburn 2-6-4 tanks on these trains. However a few remained for peak services such as this evening train to Kilmacolm, seen leaving Glasgow (St. Enoch) behind No.42057 on 19 September 1961.

The last regular use of the Fairburn 2-6-4 tanks was on the Glasgow–Gourock peak hour services pending the electrification of this busy route. On a stormy evening in April 1965 woebegone No.42241 makes a rousing start out of Paisley with a Gourock–Glasgow train.

The only Stanier 2-6-2 tanks to work in Scotland were a handful that worked on the suburban services through Glasgow Central (Low Level). When these workings were reduced and reorganised in the late 1950s most of them were transferred south, but two or three, including Nos.40150 and 40151 went to Dumfries for a while. No.40151 leaves Dumfries in August 1958 with a local train to Kirkcudbright.

After a spell of two years at Dumfries, No.40151 was moved north again for a short time and is seen here waiting to leave Muirkirk in October 1960 with a stopping train to Lanark and Carstairs. At this date it was the only survivor of the class in Scotland.

Overleaf: the ex-Caledonian Mackintosh 3F 0-6-0s of the '812' class of 1899 must have put in a lot of hard work in South and Central Scotland over the years. Ironically many of them finished their days on the metals of the rival G & SW where they were well liked. In November 1960 No.57580 coasts off the Mauchline route at Annbank with a load of coal from Kirkconnel bound for Ayr Harbour.

Ex-Caley 3F No.57577 passing Garrochburn signalbox on 24 April 1962 with Kilmarnock trip working K92—empties from Hurlford mineral sidings to Mauchline Colliery. This train was handed over to the NCB at Garrochburn sidings and worked down to Mauchline Colliery by one of their own engines. The colliery is now closed, with the sidings and box at Garrochburn demolished.

The Pickersgill '294' class of Caledonian 0-6-0s of 1918 were neither as numerous, nor in most cases as long-lived, as their Mackintosh predecessors. However a handful survived into the 1960s such as No.57661 seen here at Maxwellton with the industrial shunt from Dumfries on 25 June 1963. This photograph is taken on the only surviving remnant of the Port Road from Dumfries to Stranraer, now reduced to a single line serving various factories on the western outskirts of Dumfries.

Two very different generations of goods engines at Dalrymple Junction in 1958. Drummond Caledonian 0-6-0 No.57382 climbs the last yards to the summit with a Girvan–Ayr goods, while Austerity 2-8-0 No.90319 waits on the Dalmellington line with a heavy coal train from Waterside to Ayr Harbour.

Dumfries seemed to specialise in odd Caledonian 0-6-0s, as witness this photo of No.57302 shunting the goods yard there in June 1963. This was one of the Drummond 2F class of 1883, of which there were very few survivors by this date. More unusually it was one of a handful fitted with a flanged funnel, most of the rest of the class having a stovepipe design.

The Drummond 2F 0-6-0s were very long lived and in Ayrshire at any rate several survived until 1963. When this photograph of No.57364 was taken at Annbank in 1958 they were plentiful on the shorter mineral workings such as this one from some of the pits near Drongan to Falkland Junction (Ayr).

At the beginning of the decade 1958-67 there were a few ex-Caledonian 0-4-4 tanks still at work in Scotland, mainly as station pilots at such places as St. Enoch, Edinburgh (Princes Street) and Ayr. One of the Princes Street pilots, No.55124 of the Mackintosh 1895 batch, was specially cleaned up to work a Branch Line Society special in September 1961. The train is seen returning from Broughton (then the terminus of the Symington–Peebles line) to Edinburgh shortly after a stop at Biggar.

The famous Caledonian Single No.123 in Dr. Findlay country. On Good Friday, 12 April 1963 a train chartered by the S.L.S. pauses in Callander station in a brief spell of sunshine, shortly before a blizzard of alarming ferocity caught it in Glen Ogle, causing all concerned some anxious minutes as despite the relatively light load of the two restored Caledonian coaches the 4-2-2 nearly slipped to a standstill.

Another of the preserved Scottish quartet on its last public appearance before going into the Glasgow Transport Museum; ex-GNSR 4-4-0 No.49 *Gordon Highlander* passing through the cutting near the closed station of Carnwath on 16 October 1965 with a Branch Line Society special that toured some of the lines between Glasgow and Edinburgh

In August 1965 the centenary of the Highland Railway was commemorated by Scottish Region in a most imaginative way. The preserved Jones Goods 4-6-0 was worked to Inverness with the two restored Caledonian Grampian corridor coaches and they spent much of the last week in August running trips between Inverness and Forres. The train returned to Glasgow, 30 August on a typical Highland day of sunshine and showers, and is seen here approaching Slochd Summit from the north.

Preserved, but not at the time steamable, nor thought likely to be. By dint of hard work LNER D49 Class 4-4-0 No.246 *Morayshire* appeared under its own power for the 1975 Shildon Cavalcade. The locomotive was in the process of being moved from Ardeer to the Navy's Queen Elizabeth Yard near Dalmeny and is seen here at Dalmeny Junction being towed by a Clayton Class 17 D.8575 on 16 April 1966.

Possibly the best known preserved locomotive of them all—A3 No.4472, waiting at the east end of Edinburgh (Waverley) prior to taking over an excursion returning from Inverkeithing to Northallerton in June 1966. This view shows the corridor tender fitted to the A4s and some of the A3s for the London – Edinburgh non-stop workings.

The 'swan song' of the famous Gresley A4 Pacifics came in the years 1963-1965 when along with some A3s they held a virtual monopoly of the Glasgow (Buchanan Street)–Aberdeen expresses. This ironically was the sort of task they were designed for: relatively light smartly-timed trains over a line with only short, if in some cases sharp, gradients. A frosty 2 March 1963 finds No.60012 *Commonwealth of Australia* heading north through Bridge of Allan on the morning Glasgow–Aberdeen express.

No.60004 *William Whitelaw* heading through the notorious Blackfaulds cutting on the G & SW main line near Polquhap summit with the R.C.T.S. 'Three Summits Rail-tour' of 30 June 1963. At this time the use of A4s on the Nith Valley line was not confined to special trains, as they cropped up occasionally on through extras from Leeds at week-ends.

One of the stranger events in locomotive preservation occurred on 17 May 1967 when No.4498 *Sir Nigel Gresley* was worked north after an overhaul at Crewe Works for a special working in Scotland. BR decided to make her 'pay her passage' and she was used on the afternoon Carlisle/Perth parcels as far as Motherwell. The train is seen here passing Beattock Summit.

On 25 March 1967 Scottish Region ran a Round Scotland Rail-tour, comprising a train of seventeen coaches and taking in points as far apart as Carlisle and Aberdeen. The train was diesel worked apart from the Perth–Aberdeen section where A4 No.60009 and Class 5 No.44997 were used. The interesting thing was that *Union of South Africa* had by this time been sold to John Cameron, and BR had to ask if they could please borrow it back for the occasion! The pair are seen here waiting in Perth to take over for the run to Aberdeen.

A1 No.60140 *Balmoral* and B1 No.61231 run light into Millerhill yard to take over southbound goods trains, including the thrice weekly P.D.L. Special from Dundee to London. This photograph was taken off the footplate of V2 No.60816 that had worked this container train in from Dundee on 7 May 1964.

Under a sky of fluffy clouds A1 No.60142 *Edward Fletcher* heels to the curve through Monktonhall Junction east of Edinburgh with the 2.30 p.m. stopping train to Newcastle in September 1958. Though a light and leisurely train this was usually a Gateshead Pacific working and remained so until the end of steam on the East Coast Main Line.

Throughout 1964 A1s from Holbeck shed (Leeds) were frequent visitors to the Nith Valley Line, working north on extras and back on any service, suitable or otherwise. On Saturday 8 August No.60154 *Bon Accord* curves off the G & SW main line at Gretna Junction en route to Carlisle with the 2.0 p.m. stopping train from Glasgow (St. Enoch).

Rather surprisingly still in her original Thompson form with rimless double chimney and round dome, A2/3 No.60516 *Hycilla* coasts past Monktonhall Junction box on 7 July 1962 with an overnight parcels train from London to Edinburgh.

An A2/3 in its final form, with rimmed chimney and 'banjo' dome, on the Nith Valley Line on 4 July 1964; No.60524 *Herringbone* is on the 2.0 p.m. Glasgow (St. Enoch)–Carlisle stopping train, a duty that could be relied on to produce out of the ordinary locomotive workings. The closed station of Carronbridge is the background, with the platforms removed and the buildings in the process of conversion into a dwelling house.

An A2 aberration; No.60536 *Trimbush,* one of the Peppercorn series, built with cylinders in the conventional place and a single rimmed chimney but with a round dome, whereas the rest of the batch had 'banjo' pattern ones. The train is an excursion from Edinburgh to Bolton climbing the last bleak windy yards to Falahill Summit on the Waverley Route, 25 May 1962.

In the last decade of steam in Scotland the use of ex-LNER Pacifics on freight workings was quite common especially on the Waverley and Nith Valley routes. Peppercorn A2 No.60535 *Hornets Beauty* climbs the 1 in 100 into Blackfaulds cutting near Cumnock with the evening Hurlford (Kilmarnock)– Brent (London) fast goods on 28 May 1964. Unlike the photograph of No.60536 at Falahill, this locomotive has the conventional 'banjo' dome.

In September 1958 the vast new Millerhill marshalling yard east of Edinburgh was only at the excavation stage as can be seen in this view of A3 No.60079 *Bayardo* on an Edinburgh–Carlisle train by the Waverley Route. The locomotive is still in her original form with single chimney and round dome. It was also one of the first A3s to be withdrawn three years later, having spent much of its life based at Canal Shed (Carlisle).

By the time Leeds-based A3s had ousted the rebuilt 'Royal Scots' on many of the through workings between Leeds and Glasgow, most of them had been fitted with double chimneys which, while improving their performance, did nothing to improve their beauty; No.60070 *Gladiateur* breasts Polquhap summit south of Cumnock with an overnight St. Pancras–Glasgow (St. Enoch) sleeping car train on a cold April morning in 1961.

Corkerhill Shed (Glasgow) had no scruples about borrowing some of the Leeds A3s that had worked in from the south at summer weekends for local filling-in turns. On 22 June 1963 No.60086 *Gainsborough* finds itself leaving Ayr on a Glasgow–Girvan Saturday extra, complete with Caledonian style route indicator!

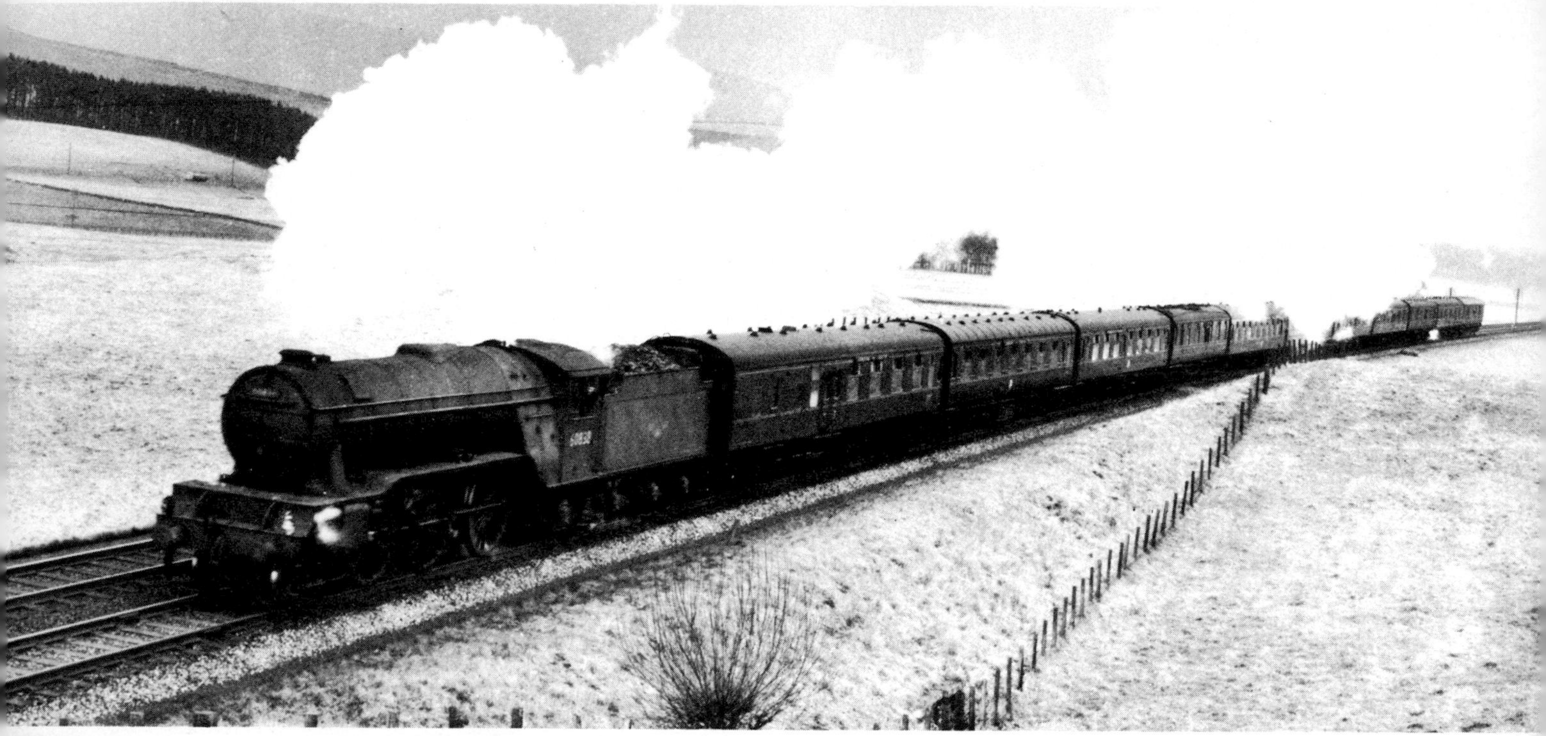
60830

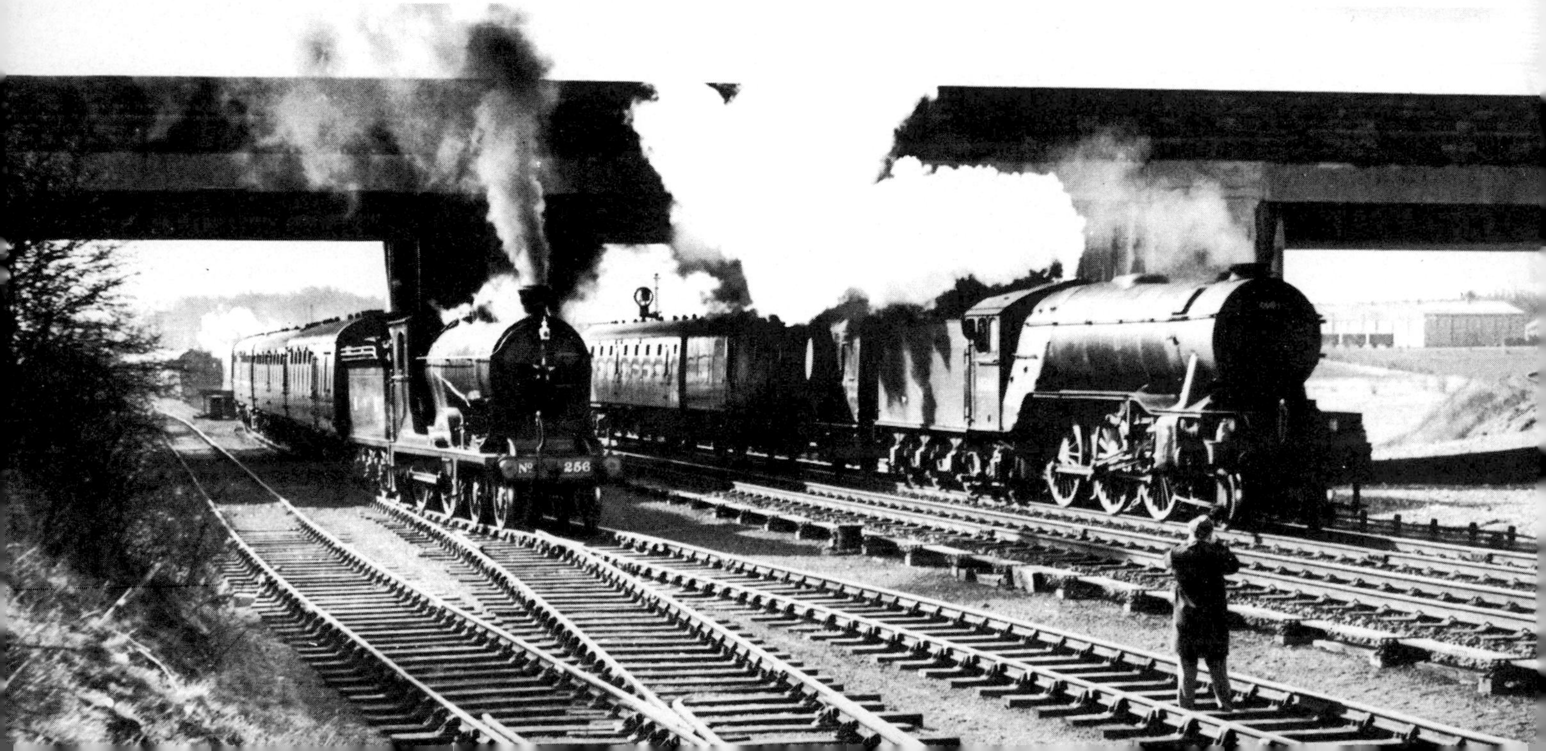
No 256

In July 1965 V2 No.60801 coasts into Perth with a morning train from Glasgow (Buchanan Street) to Dundee. This was the last year that the LNER locomotives had much share in these workings north from Glasgow, the diesels taking over completely by early 1966.

1961 the use of ex-LNER locos on the expresses between Perth and the south as far as Carlisle was not uncommon hen an LMS Pacific was not available. On a dull 4 April 1961 the morning Perth–Euston express climbs the Clyde alley near Wandel Mill (Lamington) with V2 No.60838. With an eleven coach train and a wet rail the 2-6-2 was not nding the going easy and was already somewhat late when it passed me with another ten miles to go to the summit.

2 No.60846 passing under the new road bridges on the approaches to the Forth Road Bridge on 13 March 1963, ith an express from Edinburgh to Perth via Glenfarg. On the left the preserved NB 4-4-0 No.256 *Glen Douglas* waits to scend the branch to South Queensferry with an S.L.S. excursion covering branch lines in the Edinburgh and Fife ea.

In 1962 and 1963 Ayr shed were allocated six B1s to help their over-worked stud of Black 5s. Local prejudice made them unpopular on account of deficient brakes for the harder mineral turns but they did a lot of work on passenger and fitted freight jobs. On a very frosty 18 February 1963 No.61179 removes the stock of the Carlisle–Ayr mail at the east end of Ayr station.

For all their reputation for bad brakes in Ayrshire, the B1s did some of the easier goods turns throughout the winter of 1962/63, such as this Girvan–Ayr goods seen here climbing Killochan bank with No.61243 in charge on 27 February 1963.

A B1 on its home ground. A Glasgow–Edinburgh football excursion in the little used 'suburban' platform at Waverley . . . decently screened from the main station by a high wall. The date is 16 April 1966 and the locomotive No.61029, surprisingly still sporting the name *Chamois*. By the condition of the locomotive some of the leather from this antelope could have been used to good effect.

The Reid designed Glen Class 4-4-0s of 1913 will forever be associated with the West Highland Line they were built for. By the mid 1950s B1s and Black 5s had made them redundant and they were rapidly withdrawn. One of the last survivors No.62471 *Glen Falloch* bustles through Monktonhall Junction with a short goods to North Berwick in September 1958.

The last public appearance of ex-North British Glen Class 4-4-0 No.256 before being taken into the Glasgow Transport Museum. *Glen Douglas* makes a cautious descent of the steep branch from Dalmeny Junction to South Queensferry goods station with a S.L.S. Special on Saturday 13 April 1963. The steam visible at the rear of the train is another ex-North British J37 Class No.64603, attached to work the train back up to Dalmeny.

By 1958 the only surviving mainline tank engines on the LNER lines in Scotland were the V3 2-6-2Ts. These engines of a 1939 Gresley design were never as widespread as the larger LMS 2-6-4Ts nor were they as powerful, being essentially suburban engines. Their main strongholds were the Edinburgh and Glasgow suburban services and by 1960 had been displaced from the former by dmus though they lingered on in the Glasgow area till the coming of the Blue trains in 1961. No.67617 of St. Margarets Shed (Edinburgh) hurries past Monktonhall Junction in the late summer of 1958 with a stopping train from Dunbar.

Two V3s were sent to Ayr for a very short spell early in 1961, for what reason I know not, as there were plenty of Fairburn and by then Standard 2-6-4Ts to take care of any local passenger work not in the hands of dmu's. One of the Ayr allocation, No.67616 passes Lochgreen Junction (Troon) with a train of goods vehicles en route to Barassie works for repair in March 1961. When the original batch of 'Blue trains' had to be withdrawn for modification, the V3s were recalled to the Glasgow area, from whence they were withdrawn.

The Gresley 1926 designed J39 0-6-0s were not common in Scotland, their J38 precursors being essentially built for Scottish work. However in 1958 J39 No.64986 passes Monktonhall Junction east of Edinburgh with a train of empties for the coal pits near Smeaton. The more modern lines of the J39 are in interesting contrast to the older NB-built J37's one of which is illustrated at the same spot four years later (see page 75).

On 6 July 1963 J38 No.65909 and brake van drop down the Cumbernauld Bank on the Caledonian line between Motherwell and Larbert, presumably returning to Grangemouth.

The J38 Gresley 0-6-0 was essentially a smaller-wheeled version of the J39 built with Scottish conditions very much in mind. Latterly the J38s were concentrated in Fife along with most of the remaining LNER and NB 0-6-0s. One of the Fife J38s No.65934 propels a rake of coal from Alloa Yard into the sidings at Kincardine Power Station, wreathed in a typical Firth of Forth sea mist in June 1966.

The short branch to South Queensferry goods station, almost underneath the Forth Bridge, dropped steeply from the main line at Dalmeny Junction. On 13 April 1963 when *Glen Douglas* took the S.L.S. excursion down to the bottom of the hill J37 No.64603 was attached to the rear of the train to help it up again. The 4-4-0 is out of sight behind the bridge into Dalmeny yard.

Monktonhall Junction to the east of Edinburgh was an ideal spot for locomotive variety in the late 1950s and early 1960s. Here the mainline turned away to the east while from the south and west various colliery branches and the new spur into Millerhill, not to mention the Edinburgh avoiding lines, all converged. In 1958 No.64519 takes the mainline with a rake of empties. This, to make the confusion of LNER 0-6-0s worse confounded, is a J35/4, a Reid North British design of 1906, that somehow sums up all the aesthetic short-comings of the British inside-cylindered 0-6-0.

The Reid designed 0-6-0s of 1914 were very strong, if slow, engines being intended for heavy coal working mainly in Fife and the Lothians. They were also remarkably long lived, surviving into 1966. Known in North British days as the 'S' class the LNER classified them as J37. This photograph taken on 7 July 1962 of No.64569 on coal empties for the mines round Pencaitland makes an interesting contrast with the J39 at the same place four years earlier. (See page 72).

Along with the Drummond Caledonian 0-6-0s the longest surviving pre-Grouping Scottish locomotives were the Holmes 1888 designed 0-6-0s classified J36 by the LNER. No.65288 of Thornton Shed (Fife) shunts at Manor Powis Colliery between Alloa and Stirling in June 1966. The smokebox door shows signs of the scorching that was a fault of these engines in their declining years.

Not content with surviving till the end of steam in Scotland at the end of 1966 this J36 happily worked on for three months beyond it! Thornton Shed used it for shunting the large and busy Seafield Colliery on the Fife coast as the Clayton Class 17s provided as replacements were not up to the job. This photograph on 23 March 1967 shows No.65345 happily at work at Seafield a week before 'Authority' got to hear of this practice, and put a stop to it by providing a Class 37 to take the 80 year old steam locomotive's place. No.65345 was known at Thornton as 'Dr. Findlay's engine' as it had taken part in the T.V. series about the good doctor.

Overleaf: the Scottish Region did not love its 'Britannias' but by the middle 1960s they had to use them as there was little else. No.70037 *Hereward the Wake* pulls out of Carstairs yard past Strawfrank Junction on 15 May 1964 with a goods train for Carlisle containing a ballast cleaning machine. With the coming of electrification the layout at Carstairs has altered out of all recognition and Strawfrank box has been demolished.

'Britannia' off the beaten track. No. 70009 *Alfred the Great* restarts an evening Ayr–Kilmarnock local out of Prestwick on 22 September 1966, replacing a failed rail-bus. The 'Britannia' in turn had failed that morning working the Euston–Stranraer boat-train and was being returned to Carlisle after attention at Ayr M.P.D.

The 'Clans' were more popular north of the Border than the 'Britannias' and up until the diesel take-over in 1962/63 worked many of the intermediate Anglo-Scottish expresses. One such, the 2.0 p.m. Glasgow–Liverpool, is seen here among the rolling hills of upper Clydesdale on 7 September 1961 with No.72001 *Clan Cameron* in charge.

No.72006 *Clan Mackenzie* speeds through Cumnock on 21 April 1962 with the 9.25 a.m. Leeds–Glasgow express. The fact that this is one of Kingmoor's five 'Clans' and the fact that the train at this time was normally a Class 45 working indicates that the diesel had failed at Carlisle.

To the best of my knowledge the last working of a 'Clan', certainly on a passenger train. On 17 February 1966 No.72006 *Clan Mackenzie,* devoid of nameplates, waits in Girvan station with the empty stock of a special from London that the Pacific had worked from Carlisle. The locomotive and stock returned to Ayr and then worked back to Carlisle the following evening.

The Standard 3 Moguls were very localised in distribution. There were some in N.E. England but most of the class went to Scotland being divided between Motherwell and Hurlford (Kilmarnock). From the outset those at Kilmarnock tended to be used as passenger engines, replacing the old but willing 2Ps. At the height of the Ayrshire miners' holidays in 1958 No.77016 waits at New Cumnock with the stock of an extra train to Glasgow.

Standard 3 Mogul No.77019 draws out of the platform at Kilmarnock with the stock of a train from Ayr on 2 August 1966. This was their last semi-regular passenger duties, working instead of the normal rail-bus service at peak holiday times, or deputising for the 'gas-boxes' when, as all too frequently happened, the latter failed.

'Little boy lost' might be a fitting title for this picture of Standard 2MT Mogul No.78051 doing some leisurely shunting at Annan with a Dumfries–Carlisle pick-up goods on 20 August 1964. There were never more than a handful of these little Moguls in Scotland, mostly at Hawick and I believe one or two based on St. Margarets (Edinburgh). No.78051 appeared in S.W. Scotland in the summer of 1964, I think by mistake. Dumfries had it for a time before sending it to Stranraer who used it on the Whithorn Branch till that closed. It then went to Ayr where it filled in doing odd jobs until all steam ceased there in October 1966.

The Standard tanks came early to Scotland and took their places alongside the established Fairburn 2-6-4Ts on the longer distance suburban trains. In 1958 No.80025, sporting the Caledonian type route indicator, restarts a Girvan - Glasgow stopping train from Dalrymple station shortly before it closed. The signal box is pure G & SW, as is the lower quadrant signal.

Two generations of passenger tank locomotive in Ayr in August 1958. Standard 2-6-4T No.80024 with Caledonian Route indicator leaves with a local train for Glasgow, while Ayr's immaculate station pilot ex-Caledonian 2PT 0-4-4T No.55262 shunts vans at an adjacent platform. The use of the down platform for Glasgow bound trains at Ayr was common in steam days, where the stock of an incoming train was re-engined and returned from the same platform to save complicated shunting movements.

In Scotland, more than England, the Standard 2-6-4 tanks were treated as mixed traffic engines as in this case with the doyen of the Class No.80000 passing through Crosshouse station with an Ardrossan – Kilmarnock goods in June 1963. The train is on the line from Irvine to Kilmarnock with the old G & SW main line via Dalry in the background. Both lines are now closed and lifted and Crosshouse station totally demolished.

THE BR STANDARD 5 4-6-0s AND STANDARD 4 2-6-0s

By the late summer of 1958 Corkerhill Shed (Glasgow) had an allocation of Standard 5s that were used to replace 'Jubilees' on some of the internal Scottish services. One such turn, the 4.20 p.m. Stranraer–Glasgow approaches Dalrymple Junction in August 1958 with No.73123 in charge, at a time when it was a toss up whether this train would be Standard 5 or 'Jubilee' worked.

Standard 5 No.73059 coasts round the curves near Ardoch in the Drumlanrigg Gorge south of Sanquhar with a southbound goods train made up of rails on 4 July 1964.

The Standard 4 Moguls were very popular in South-west Scotland and worked over most lines in the area. No.76112 drops down the Longwood Bank into Dumfries with a goods from Stranraer on 16 May 1962. This was the easternmost part of the famous 'Port Road', now alas closed.

By 1963 the Ayr–Dalmellington services were nominally rail-bus operated, on the rare occasions when they could be persuaded to start. However at the height of the summer holidays they were replaced by steam hauled trains. No.76096 heads a rake of four local coaches off the branch and onto the Girvan–Ayr lines at Dalrymple Junction on 30 July 1963. This was the last summer of passenger workings on the branch which was closed beyond Waterside the following April. Ayr had a tradition of keeping one or two steam locomotives in good condition for extra passenger workings even in the DMU epoch, and No.76096 was one of these 'pets' as they were known, that survived in good condition till the end of Ayrshire steam in October 1966.

While Caprotti Black 5s were unknown in Scotland there were several of the Standard 5s so equipped, mostly based at St. Rollox (Glasgow). Ayr not to be outdone 'borrowed' No.73134 from Patricroft (without the latter's knowledge) for most of the summer of 1965. Coupled to Class 5 No.45161 it waits to work the Euston—Stranraer boat train forward on 30 July 1965. This was the day that the 'Britannia' on the 'Paddy' had failed at Closeburn and it had been worked forward to Ayr by Class 45 D34 seen here in the old Dalmellington platform.

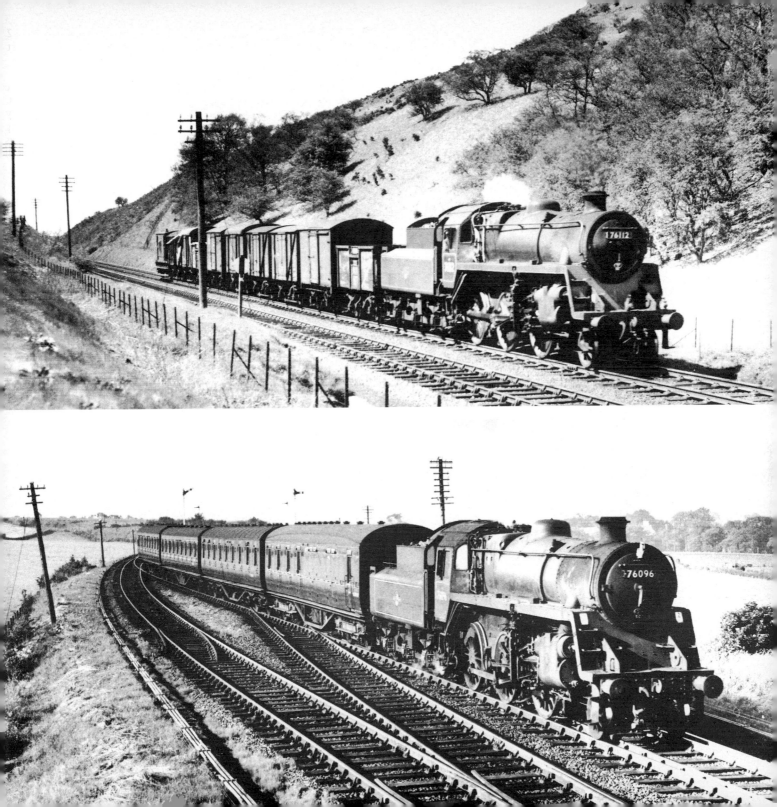

The ten-coupled Austerities were highly thought of in south Scotland just as the eight-coupled variety were not. There were never many of them and they were entirely confined to freight working between Carlisle and the industrial areas of south Glasgow with the occasional side trip up the Nith Valley. The last one ran until mid 1962 but it was in the years 1958 to 1960 that they were most in evidence in the decade under consideration. On 28 August 1958 No.90768 swings onto the Nith Valley line at Gretna Junction with a northbound goods comprising a good proportion of gunpowder vans for Ardeer.

Apart from Thornton Jnc. the other places to have a few shedded in the early 1960 epoch were Ardrossan and Ayr. The latter used them turn about with the 'Crabs' on the arduous Waterside coal trains till the early months of 1962. No.90463 rounds the long curve past the site of Smithston Junction near Patna on a crisp March day in 1961 with the first heavy morning rake of empties from Ayr Harbour to Waterside.

The eight-coupled Austerities had a longer innings, especially in Fife, where they survived until the end of Scottish based steam in December 1966. A month before this sad event Nos.90444 and 90628 wait in steam on Thornton shed (Fife) for coal workings in the Fife coalfield.

It has always been a surprise to me that the highly competent 9Fs were never shedded in Scotland, as these ten-coupled prodigies would have been ideal for lines such as the Highland or the heavy roads to Stranraer. Some of the Carlisle engines worked over the Caledonian line from time to time, mostly on trains connected with the iron works in the Motherwell area. In this August 1964 picture No.92009 comes off the Caley line at Gretna Junction with a train mainly consisting of empty iron ore hoppers. The Nith Valley line can be seen curving sharply westwards on the left hand side.

On 17 May 1967 9F No.92129 returns south with a company train (of empty tanks) seen here immediately north of Beattock station. Two points of interest are the smoke clinging around the smokebox in the best 'Duchess' fashion, when a big boilered engine was fired while coasting. More alarming is the nearly empty tender, as by this time while some of the Scottish sheds had water and turning facilities virtually none had coal, and engines working north from Carlisle had to have enough on the tender for the return journey . . . which in this case looks like going to be a damned close run thing! By September of this year all steam working to and from Scotland had ceased, but it is fitting that the engines most involved in these final days should be the ultimate class of British steam locomotive.

Ayr M.P.D. did not like 'North British injuins' in any shape or form. Not long before the B1s arrived in 1962, two J37s were sent there with disastrous results . . . one was sent to Waterside and failed before it got there and the other to Bargany and failed on the way back. They then lay at the back of the shed for two years, before being taken to the West of Scotland Shipbreaking yard at Troon for cutting up. No.64626 makes its last journey in company with two condemned Caley 0-6-0s near Troon on 20 May 1964.